# Creative IDEAS

*Second Edition*

## Student Activity Book

### Book 2
### Language Level:
### Beginning

By
Anita Canul, Julia Ebey Hughes, Solveig Villicaña,
Walter Thurston, Wanda Ballard, and Phyllis Tighe

Ballard & Tighe

LISTENING  SPEAKING  READING  WRITING

**An IDEA® Language Development Program from Ballard & Tighe**

Managing Editor: Patrice Gotsch
Project Editor: Linda Mammano
Editorial Staff: Kristin Belsher, Michelle Martinez, and Rebecca Ratnam
Graphic Designer: Tina Rose
Art Director: Danielle Arreola
Contributing Writers (Creative Beats): Patrice Gotsch and Linda Mammano
Printing Coordinator: Cathy Sanchez
Art Credits: [Photodisc]/[Photodisc Blue]/Getty Images: front cover, 2, 16, 27, 40, 50, 56, 97

2009 Printing
ISBN 978-1-55501-988-4 • Catalog #3-082

# CREATIVE IDEAS
## TABLE OF CONTENTS

# INTRODUCTION

*Creative IDEAS* Student Activity Book 2 provides exercises that reinforce the vocabulary and concepts introduced in Unit 2 of the *Carousel of IDEAS*, 4th Edition program. After receiving instruction in *Carousel*, students can practice what they learned by completing the corresponding exercises in *Creative IDEAS*. These exercises are varied and interesting, yet fit into broad classifications that students will understand and find familiar as they progress through the book.

Listening, speaking, reading, and writing exercises are integrated throughout *Creative IDEAS*. Vocabulary and concepts are continually reviewed and reinforced so that students retain what they learn. In addition to building their language skills, students using *Creative IDEAS* also build cognitive skills as they complete puzzles, match sentences and pictures, identify and classify words and concepts, and create original writing.

A corresponding audio CD is available with each *Creative IDEAS* Student Activity Book. These CDs accompany the listening activities in the books, including the newest feature—Creative Beats—which help students improve their speaking skills in a fun, stress-free way.

The title of each lesson conveys the desired process and purpose. The following are the major lessons in *Creative IDEAS*:

**Identify:** All new vocabulary and concepts related to the target topic are introduced in the **Identify** lessons.

**Build Up:** The **Build Up** lessons reinforce the language introduced on the **Identify** pages. Students look at stimulus pictures and then listen to and repeat target sentences. Some of the **Build Up** lessons feature an audio component, which is indicated by the graphic of a compact disc positioned next to the lesson heading. The audio CD may be purchased with this book, or the instructor can administer these listening lessons to the students.

**Cut Up:** In these lessons, students cut out pictures and paste them by the corresponding sentences. For students not yet able to read, the adjacent **Match Up** lesson provides a model for students to follow.

**Match Up:** In these lessons, students match pictures and then write each target vocabulary word.

**Review:** These lessons review what students have learned about the target topic. Lessons usually integrate the audio CD. As in the **Build Up** lesson, students listen to the target sentence and repeat it. As an extension, students then write the target sentence. Students who are not yet able to write full sentences may write the target word only. (NOTE: The **Build Up** and **Review** lessons frequently use the same CD track.)

**Creative Beat:** In these lessons, students refine their speaking skills in a fun and engaging way. Each unique Creative Beat reinforces level-appropriate vocabulary and concepts while exposing students to the rhythms of natural speech. The accompanying audio is provided on the CD.

> **NOTE: Teachers should read the teacher directions at the bottom of the page before having students start each lesson.**

This *Creative IDEAS* Student Activity Book is intended for individual use; each student should have his or her own copy. Even though *Creative IDEAS* functions as an excellent accompaniment to the *Carousel of IDEAS*, 4th Edition program, these books also can supplement other ESL/ELD programs. **This book is fully copyrighted and cannot be reproduced.**

# IDENTIFY
## At Home

### grandfather

_____

- - - - - - - - - - - - - - - -

_____

### grandmother

_____

- - - - - - - - - - - - - - - -

_____

### cousin

_____

- - - - - - - - - - - - - - - -

_____

### aunt

_____

- - - - - - - - - - - - - - - -

_____

### uncle

_____

- - - - - - - - - - - - - - - -

_____

*(continued on next page)*

**Teacher:** Instruct students to identify and write the names of the people in the family.

# IDENTIFY
## At School

secretary

_____

---------------------------

_____

principal

_____

---------------------------

_____

custodian

_____

---------------------------

_____

nurse

_____

---------------------------

_____

**Teacher:** Instruct students to identify and write the names of the people at school.

1

# BUILD UP
## Listen and Repeat

These are people at home and at school.

1.  She's the **grandmother**.

2.  He's the **grandfather**.

3.  She's the **aunt**.

## Make the sentences:

4. uncle

5. cousin

6. principal

7. custodian

8. secretary

9. nurse

*(continued on next page)*

**Teacher:** Instruct students to listen to and repeat the sentences. Use the Book 2 CD, Track 1, or have students repeat after you. For items 4–9 and 13–22, students should use the key words to create sentences that are modeled after the sentences they just heard and repeated.

# BUILD UP
## Listen  and Repeat

These are things at school.  What do you see?

10.     I see the **ruler**.

11.     I see the **CD player**.

12.     I see the **page**.

## Make the sentences:

13. library          14. bench          15. board

# BUILD UP
## Listen  and Repeat

16. bulletin board

17. drinking fountain

18. wastebasket

19. scissors

20. office

21. glue

22. bars

# CUT UP

1. This is the **principal**.

2. This is the **custodian**.

3. This is the **nurse**.

4. This is the **secretary**.

**Teacher:** Instruct students to cut out each picture, and paste it in the box next to the sentence it matches.

# MATCH UP

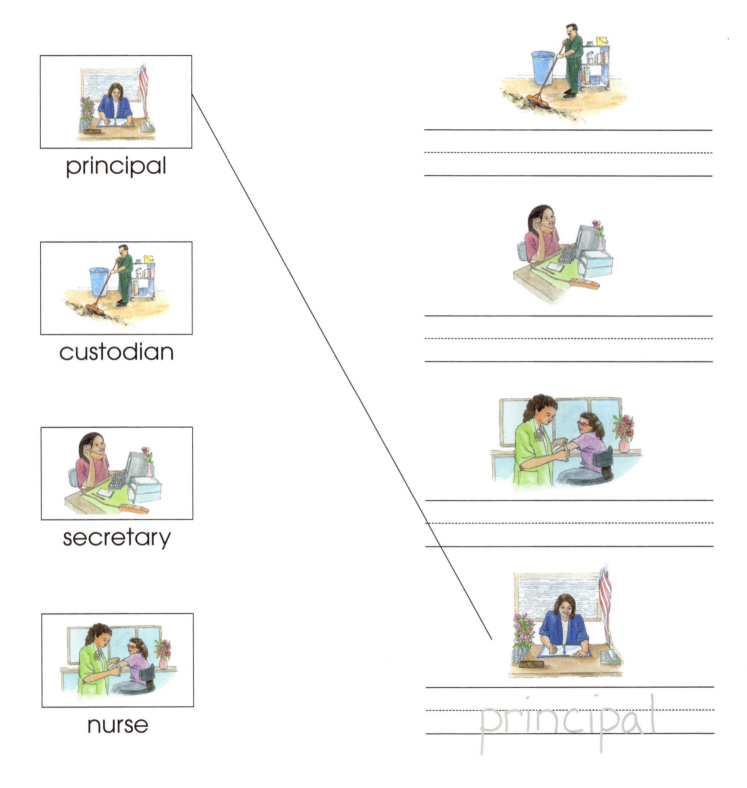

principal

custodian

secretary

nurse

principal

**Teacher:** Instruct students to draw lines to connect the matching pictures, and then write the words.

# CUT UP

1. This is the **grandmother**.

2. This is the **grandfather**.

3. This is the **aunt**.

4. This is the **uncle**.

5. This is the **cousin**.

✂ - - - - - - - - - - - - - - - - - - - - - - - - - - - - - - - - - - - - - - - - - - - - - - - - - - - - -

**Teacher:** Instruct students to cut out each picture, and paste it in the box next to the sentence it matches.

# MATCH UP

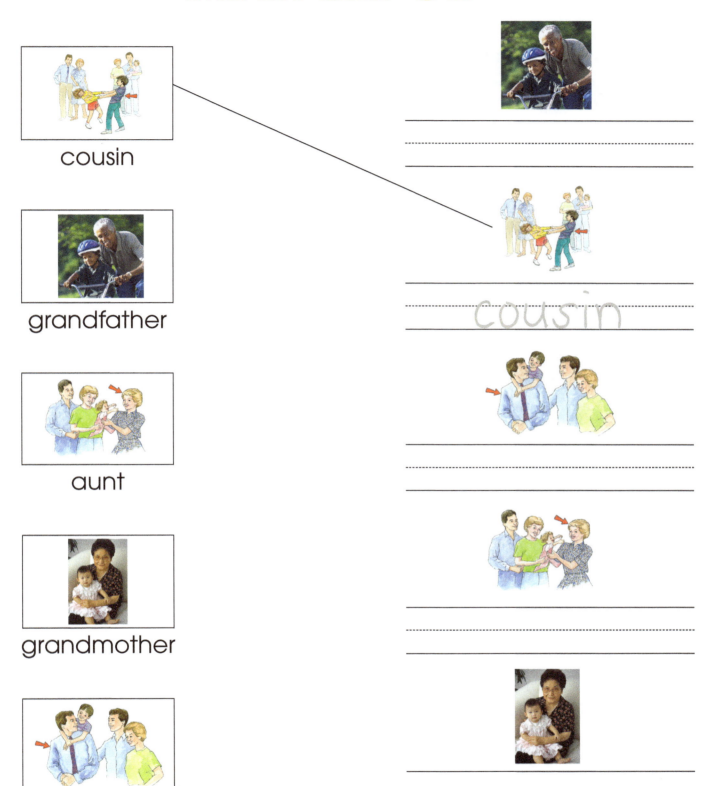

cousin

grandfather

aunt

grandmother

uncle

cousin

**Teacher:** Instruct students to draw lines to connect the matching pictures, and then write the words.

# ALL ABOUT MY SCHOOL

This is my **teacher**.

This is our **principal**.

This is our **secretary**.

This is our **custodian**.

This is our **nurse**.

**Teacher:** Instruct students to write the key words or sentences (whichever you choose) on p. 15, and then draw a picture to go with each sentence.

14

ALL ABOUT MY SCHOOL PEOPLE

_____

- - - - - - - - - - - - - - - - - - - - - - - - - -

_____

_____

- - - - - - - - - - - - - - - - - - - - - - - - - -

_____

_____

- - - - - - - - - - - - - - - - - - - - - - - - - -

_____

_____

- - - - - - - - - - - - - - - - - - - - - - - - - -

_____

_____

- - - - - - - - - - - - - - - - - - - - - - - - - -

_____

# CREATIVE BEAT

## Where Are the People in Your Family?

Where are the people in your family?
In my family?
Yes, in your family.


My grandma is Jane.
She lives in Maine.

My grandpa is Joe.
He lives in Idaho.

My uncle is Roy.
He lives in Illinois.

My aunt is Flo.
She lives in Mexico.

My cousin is Anna.
She lives in Montana.


Where are the people in *your* family?
In *my* family?
Yes, in your family.

**Teacher:** Have students listen to the Creative Beat twice. Use the Book 2 CD, Track 2, or read the lyrics aloud. If students are able, have them recite the beat along with the CD or with you. Encourage students to use hand and body motions that correspond to the lyrics.

# IDENTIFY

board

_____

- - - - - - - - - - - -

office

_____

- - - - - - - - - - - -

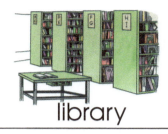

library

_____

- - - - - - - - - - - -

scissors

_____

- - - - - - - - - - - -

bars

_____

- - - - - - - - - - - -

ruler

_____

- - - - - - - - - - - -

glue

_____

- - - - - - - - - - - -

page

_____

- - - - - - - - - - - -

bench

_____

- - - - - - - - - - - -

wastebasket

_____

- - - - - - - - - - - -

CD player

_____

- - - - - - - - - - - -

drinking fountain

_____

- - - - - - - - - - - -

bulletin board

_____

- - - - - - - - - - - -

**Teacher:** Instruct students to identify and write the names of the things at school.

# BUILD UP

We have a bulletin board.

1. We have a board.

2. We have

3. 

4. 

5. 

6. We have scissors.

7. We have

8. 

board

ruler

page

bench

library

scissors

glue

bars

**Teacher:** Instruct students to write sentences using the key words.

# MATCH UP

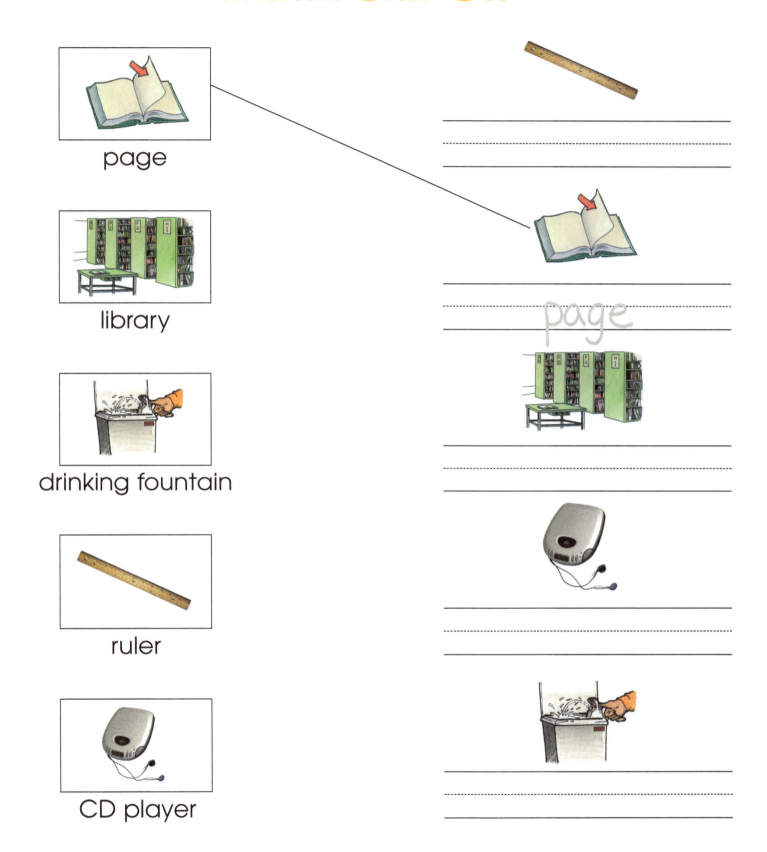

page

library

drinking fountain

ruler

CD player

page

**Teacher:** Instruct students to draw lines to connect the matching pictures, and then write the words.

# CUT UP

1.  I see a **board**.

2.  I see a **wastebasket**.

3.  I see a **ruler**.

4.  I see a **page**.

5.  I see a **bench**.

**Teacher:** Instruct students to cut out each picture, and paste it in the box next to the sentence it matches.

# MATCH UP

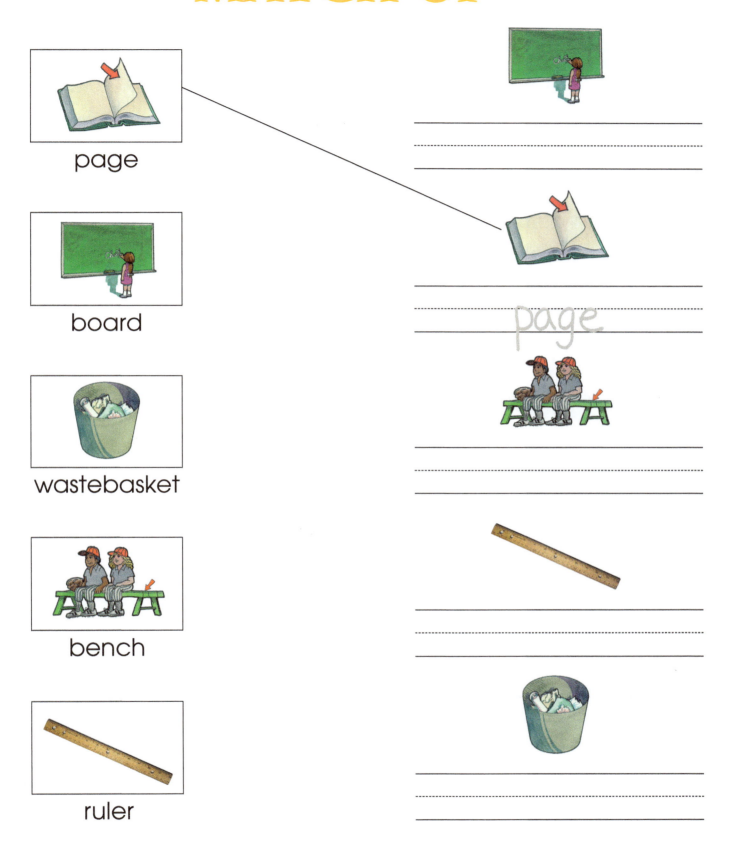

page

board

wastebasket

bench

ruler

page

**Teacher:** Instruct students to draw lines to connect the matching pictures, and then write the words.

# CUT UP

1. I see a **bulletin board**.

2. I see an **office**.

3. I see some **scissors**.

4. I see some **glue**.

5. I see some **bars**.

**Teacher:** Instruct students to cut out each picture, and paste it in the box next to the sentence it matches.

# MATCH UP

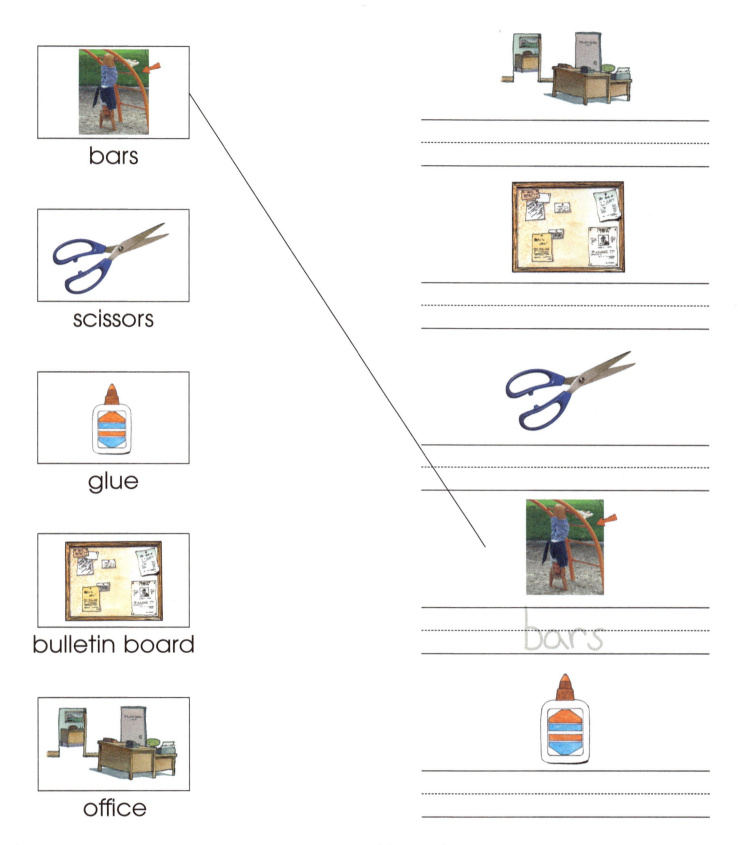

bars

scissors

glue

bulletin board

office

bars

**Teacher:** Instruct students to draw lines to connect the matching pictures, and then write the words.

# REVIEW

1

Listen,  Repeat, and Write

These are people at home and at school.

1. She's the **grandmother**.

2. He's the **grandfather**.

3. She's the **aunt**.

## Make the sentences:

4. uncle

5. cousin

6. principal

7. custodian

8. secretary

9. nurse

**Teacher:** Instruct students to listen to, repeat, and write the sentences. Use the Book 2 CD, Track 1, or have students repeat after you. **If using the CD, press the pause button when you hear the beep and instruct students to write the sentence or key word. When students are finished writing, resume the CD.** For items 4–9 and 13–22, students create their own sentences orally, but write the key words only.

# REVIEW

## Listen, Repeat, and Write

These are things at school.  What do you see?

10.  I see the **ruler**.

11.  I see the **CD player**.

12.  I see the **page**.

## Make the sentences:

13.  library

14.  bench

15.  board

*(continued on next page)*

# REVIEW

Listen,  Repeat,  and Write

16. bulletin board

_____

_____

17. drinking fountain

_____

_____

18. wastebasket

_____

_____

19. scissors

_____

_____

20. office

_____

_____

21. glue

_____

_____

22. bars

_____

_____

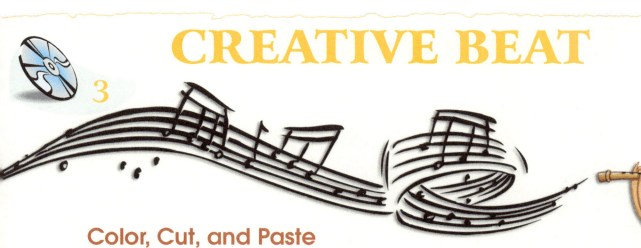

## Color, Cut, and Paste

Color the picture of the animal
brown, yellow, and red.
Cut out the picture with scissors.
That's what my teacher says.

So I color a little bird
brown, yellow, and red.
I cut out the picture with scissors
just like my teacher says.

Paste the picture of the animal
colored brown, yellow, and red.
Paste it on the cover of your book.
That's what my teacher says.

I look at the picture I made.
My bird is brown, yellow, and red.
What an excellent picture!
That's what my teacher says.

**Teacher:** Have students listen to the Creative Beat twice. Use the Book 2 CD, Track 3, or read the lyrics aloud. If students are able, have them recite the beat along with the CD or with you. Encourage students to use hand and body motions that correspond to the lyrics.

# IDENTIFY

**11** ·:::::·
eleven
_____
- - - - - - - - - - - - - - - - - -
_____

**12** ·:::::
twelve
_____
- - - - - - - - - - - - - - - - - -
_____

**13** ·:::::·
thirteen
_____
- - - - - - - - - - - - - - - - - -
_____

**14** ·:::::·
fourteen
_____
- - - - - - - - - - - - - - - - - -
_____

**15** ·:::::·
fifteen
_____
- - - - - - - - - - - - - - - - - -
_____

**16** ·::::::·
sixteen
_____
- - - - - - - - - - - - - - - - - -
_____

**17** ·::::::·
seventeen
_____
- - - - - - - - - - - - - - - - - -
_____

**18** ·::::::·
eighteen
_____
- - - - - - - - - - - - - - - - - -
_____

**19** ·::::::·
nineteen
_____
- - - - - - - - - - - - - - - - - -
_____

**20** ·::::::·
twenty
_____
- - - - - - - - - - - - - - - - - -
_____

**Teacher:** Instruct students to identify and write the number words.

# DRAW IT

Draw 16 green ▲s.

Draw 20 red ♥s.

Draw 18 yellow ☾s.

Draw 17 blue ◯s.

**Teacher:** Instruct students to draw and color the objects as directed.

# MATCH UP

**11** eleven

**12** twelve

**13** thirteen

**14** fourteen

**15** fifteen

eleven

**Teacher:** Instruct students to draw lines to connect the matching numerals and number concepts, and then write the words.

# MATCH UP

**16**

sixteen

**17**

seventeen

**18**

eighteen

**19**

nineteen

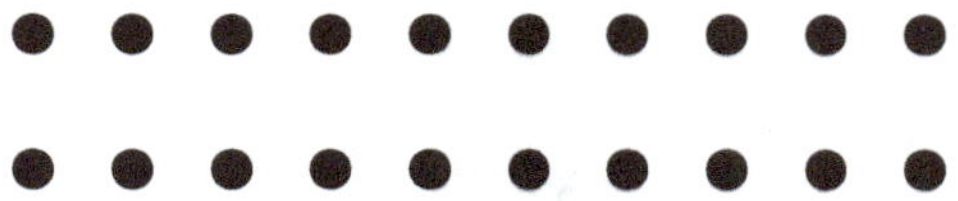

**20**

twenty

31

# IDENTIFY

bird

cat

monkey

kitten

rabbit

puppy

dog

fish

turtle

mouse

**Teacher:** Instruct students to identify and write the names of the animals.

# BUILD UP
## Listen  and Repeat

4

These are pets. What do you see?

1.   I see a **dog**.

2. I see a **cat**.

3. I see a **kitten**.

## Make the sentences:

4. bird

5. puppy

6. fish

7. rabbit

8. turtle

9. mouse

*(continued on next page)*

**Teacher:** Instruct students to listen to and repeat the sentences. Use the Book 2 CD, Track 4, or have students repeat after you. For items 4–9 and 13–18, students should use the key words to create sentences that are modeled after the sentences they just heard and repeated.

# BUILD UP
## Listen  and Repeat

These are foods.  What do you want?

10.  I want some **grapes**.

11.  I want an **apple**.

12.  I want a **potato**.

## Make the sentences:

13. pear

14. banana

15. tomato

16. carrot

17. lemon

18. pineapple

# BUILD UP

 We like the cat.

1. We like the dog.

        dog

2. We like the

        puppy

3.

        monkey

4.

        turtle

5.

        fish

6.

        rabbit

7.

        bird

        ?

I like the

**Teacher:** Instruct students to write sentences using the key words. Students choose their favorite pet for the last item.

# CUT UP

1.  I see a **kitten**.

2.  I see a **cat**.

3.  I see a **turtle**.

4.  I see a **fish**.

5.  I see a **mouse**.

**Teacher:** Instruct students to cut out each picture, and paste it in the box next to the sentence it matches.

# MATCH UP

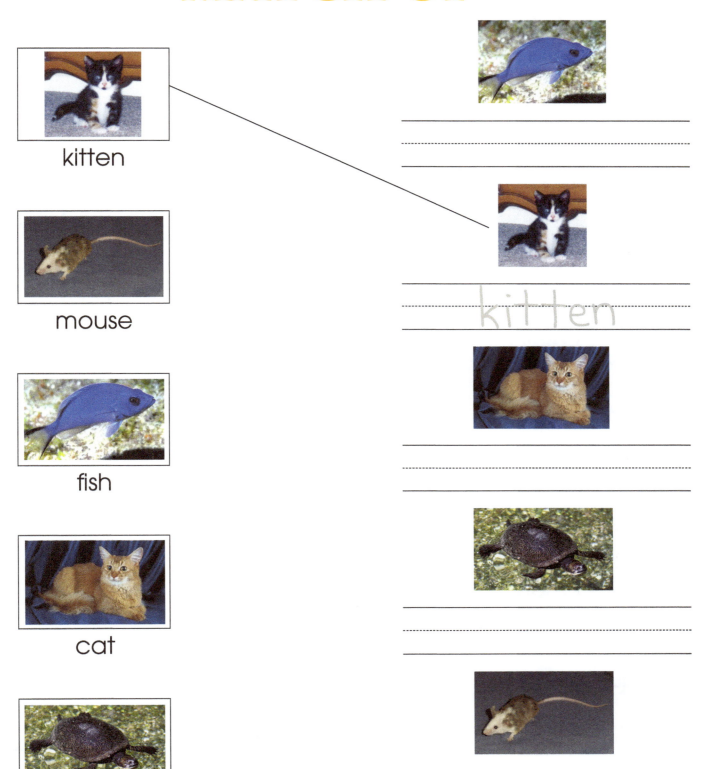

kitten

mouse

fish

cat

turtle

kitten

**Teacher:** Instruct students to draw lines to connect the matching pictures, and then write the words.

# CUT UP

1.  I see a **puppy**.

2.  I see a **rabbit**.

3.  I see a **bird**.

4.  I see a **dog**.

5.  I see a **monkey**.

✂ — — — — — — — — — — — — — — — — — — — — — — — —

**Teacher:** Instruct students to cut out each picture, and paste it in the box next to the sentence it matches.

# MATCH UP

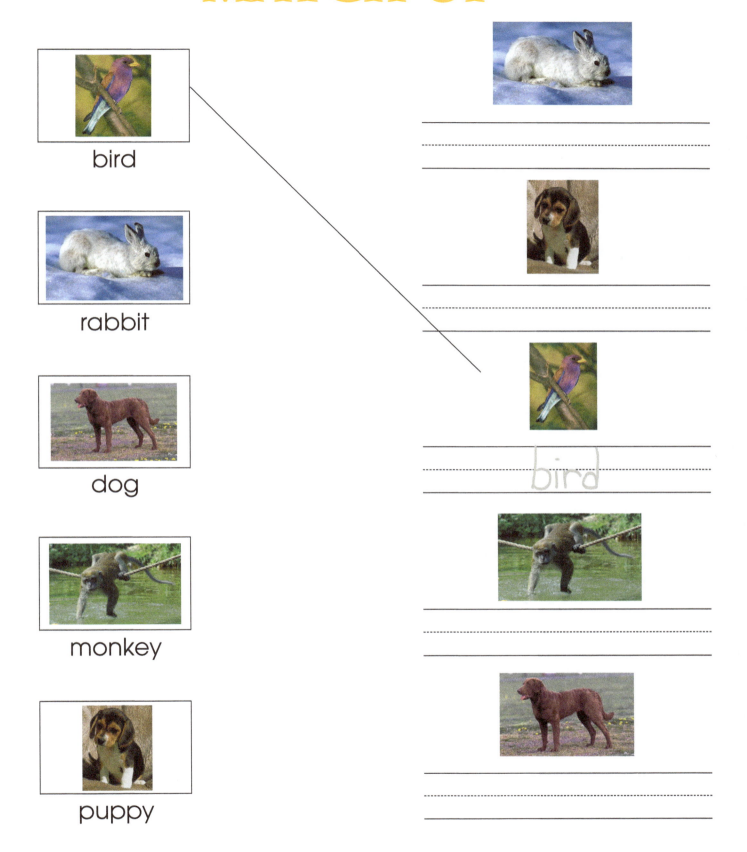

bird

rabbit

dog

monkey

puppy

bird

**Teacher:** Instruct students to draw lines to connect the matching pictures, and then write the words.

# CREATIVE BEAT

### I See Three

Look!  Look!
Three monkeys inside the cage.
One, two, three.
Three monkeys I see.

Look!  Look!
Three turtles on top of the table.
One, two, three.
Three turtles I see.

Look!  Look!
Three kittens in a row.
One, two, three.
Three kittens I see.

Look!  Look!
Three puppies in front of the house.
One, two, three.
Three puppies I see.

Look!  Look!
Three cats under the bed.
One, two, three.
Three cats I see.

**Teacher:**  Have students listen to the Creative Beat twice. Use the Book 2 CD, Track 5, or read the lyrics aloud. If students are able, have them recite the beat along with the CD or with you. Encourage students to use hand and body motions that correspond to the lyrics.

# IDENTIFY

## Fruits

pineapple

_____

- - - - - - - - - - - - - -

_____

pear

_____

- - - - - - - - - - - - - -

_____

grapes

_____

- - - - - - - - - - - - - -

_____

banana

_____

- - - - - - - - - - - - - -

_____

orange

_____

- - - - - - - - - - - - - -

_____

apple

_____

- - - - - - - - - - - - - -

_____

lemon

_____

- - - - - - - - - - - - - -

_____

## Vegetables

carrot

_____

- - - - - - - - - - - - - -

_____

potato

_____

- - - - - - - - - - - - - -

_____

tomato

_____

- - - - - - - - - - - - - -

_____

onion

_____

- - - - - - - - - - - - - -

_____

**Teacher:** Instruct students to identify and write the names of the fruits and vegetables.

# BUILD UP

We want a pear.

1. We want a carrot.

2. We want an apple.

3. We want

4.

5.

6.

7.

I want

a carrot

an apple

an onion

a banana

an orange

a tomato

a pineapple

**Teacher:** Instruct students to write sentences using the key words. Students choose their favorite fruit or vegetable for the last item.

42

# CLASSIFY

## What goes together?  Circle the pictures.

| | | | |
|---|---|---|---|
|  |  |  |  |
| onion | potato | dog | carrot |
|  |  |  |  |
| pineapple | book | orange | leg |
|  |  |  |  |
| lemon | banana | apple | five |
|  |  |  |  |
| grapes | pear | mother | tomato |

They are all ___foods___.

**Teacher:**  Instruct students to circle the pictures on the page that go together. Then have students write the words below the pictures they have circled.

# CUT UP

1. I want a **potato**.

2. I want a **banana**.

3. I want a **lemon**.

4. I want a **tomato**.

5. I want a **pineapple**.

6. I want a **pear**.

**Teacher:** Instruct students to cut out each picture, and paste it in the box next to the sentence it matches.

# MATCH UP

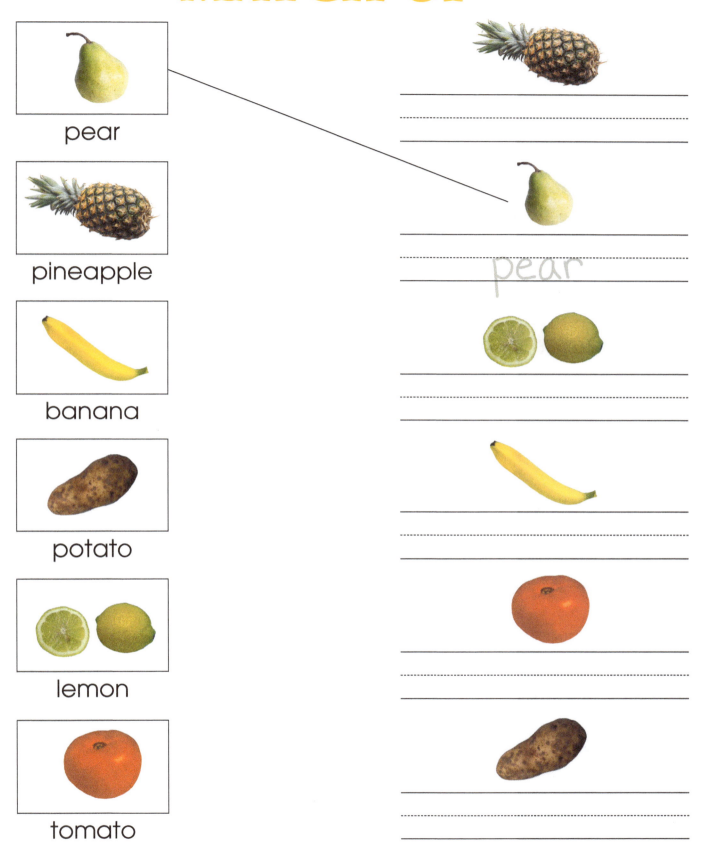

pear

pineapple

banana

potato

lemon

tomato

pear

**Teacher:** Instruct students to draw lines to connect the matching pictures, and then write the words.

# CUT UP

1. I want a **carrot**.

2. I want an **apple**.

3. I want an **orange**.

4. I want an **onion**.

5. I want some **grapes**.

**Teacher:** Instruct students to cut out each picture, and paste it in the box next to the sentence it matches.

# MATCH UP

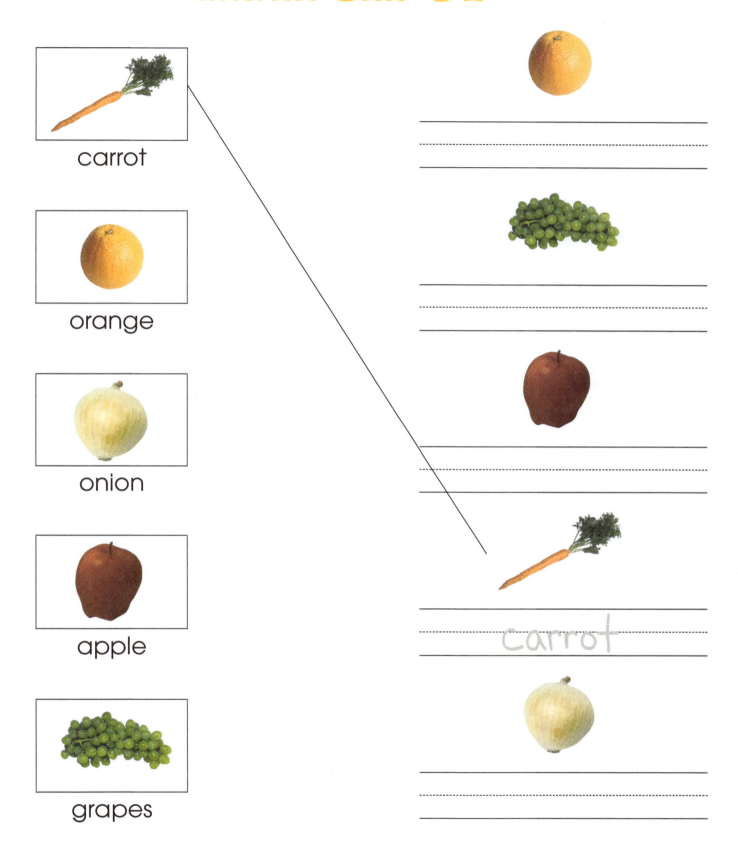

carrot

orange

onion

apple

grapes

carrot

**Teacher:** Instruct students to draw lines to connect the matching pictures, and then write the words.

# REVIEW

4

Listen,  Repeat, and Write

These are pets. What do you see?

1. I see a **dog**.

_____

2. I see a **cat**.

_____

3. I see a **kitten**.

_____

## Make the sentences:

4. bird

_____

5. puppy

_____

6. fish

_____

7. rabbit

_____

8. turtle

_____

9. mouse

_____

**Teacher:** Instruct students to listen to, repeat, and write the sentences. Use the Book 2 CD, Track 4, or have students repeat after you. **If using the CD, press the pause button when you hear the beep and instruct students to write the sentence or key word. When students are finished writing, resume the CD.** For items 4–9 and 13–18, students create their own sentences orally, but write the key words only.

# REVIEW
## Listen, 👂 Repeat, 👄 and Write ✏️

4

These are foods.  What do you want?

10.      I want some **grapes**.

11.      I want an **apple**.

12.      I want a **potato**.

## Make the sentences:

13. pear

14. banana

15. tomato

16. carrot

17. lemon

18. pineapple

# CREATIVE BEAT

### Do You Like Fruit?

Do you like fruit?
I sure do!
I like bananas.
I like apples.
I like grapes.
I like pineapples.

Do you like vegetables?
I sure do!
I like onions.
I like potatoes.
I like carrots.
I like tomatoes.

What about pears?
Do you like those, too?
I sure do!
What about you?

**Teacher:** Have students listen to the Creative Beat twice. Use the <u>Book 2 CD, Track 6</u>, or read the lyrics aloud. If students are able, have them recite the beat along with the CD or with you. Encourage students to use hand and body motions that correspond to the lyrics.

# IDENTIFY

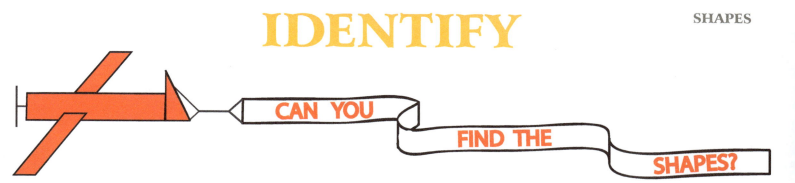

CAN YOU FIND THE SHAPES?

triangle
_____
- - - - - - - - - - - -
_____

line
_____
- - - - - - - - - - - -
_____

circle
_____
- - - - - - - - - - - -
_____

rectangle
_____
- - - - - - - - - - - -
_____

square
_____
- - - - - - - - - - - -
_____

**Teacher:** Instruct students to identify and write the names of the shapes.

# BUILD UP

## Listen  and Repeat

These are shapes.

1. It's a **triangle**.

2. It's a **square**.

Make the sentences:

3. line          4. circle          5. rectangle

These are parts of the body.

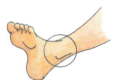

6. This is an **ankle**.

7. This is an **elbow**.

**Teacher:** Instruct students to listen to and repeat the sentences. Use the Book 2 CD, Track 7, or have students repeat after you. For items 3–5, 9–12, and 14–16, students should use the key words to create sentences that are modeled after the sentences they just heard and repeated.

# BUILD UP

7

Listen  and Repeat

8.  This is a **back**.

## Make the sentences:

9. tongue

10. shoulder

11. knee

12. wrist

13.  These are **fingers**.

## Make the sentences:

14. toes

15. lips

16. teeth

# MATCH UP

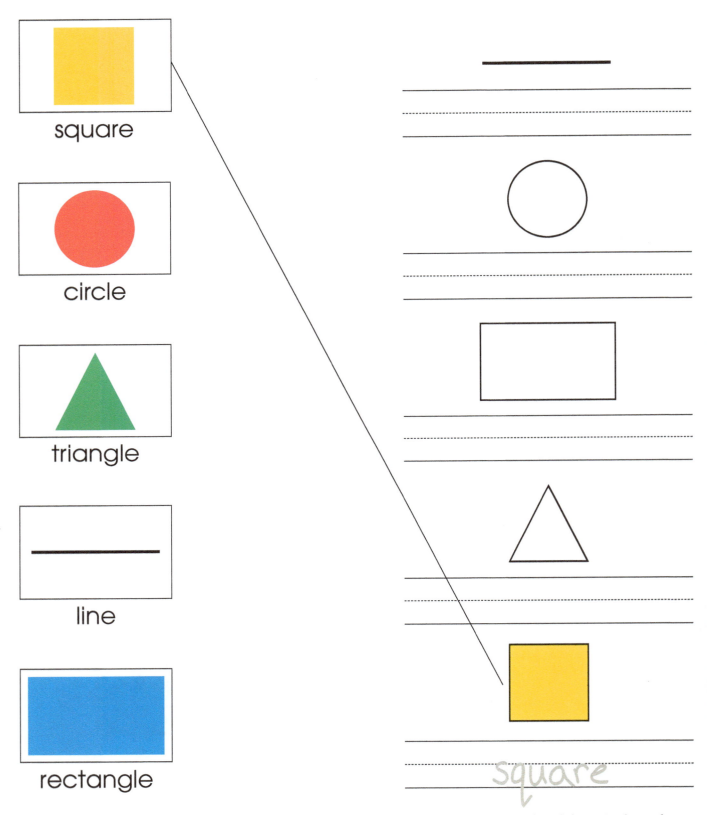

square

circle

triangle

line

rectangle

square

**Teacher:** Instruct students to draw lines to connect the matching shapes, color the shapes to match, and then write the words.

# BUILD UP

| circle | square | triangle | rectangle | line |

1. green — It's a green square.

2. brown — It's a brown circle.

3. blue

4. red

5. black

6. purple

7. yellow

**Teacher:** Instruct students to write sentences using the key color and shape words.

# CREATIVE BEAT

## Shapes Everywhere

I see shapes everywhere
when I look around.
Come along with me!
Let me show you what I found.

The ball is a circle.
The book is a square.
The paper is a rectangle.
I see shapes everywhere!

The flag is a rectangle.
The desk is a square.
The table is a circle.
There are shapes everywhere!

The pencil is a line.
The window is a square.
The sign is a triangle.
Do you see shapes everywhere?

**Teacher:** Have students listen to the Creative Beat twice. Use the Book 2 CD, Track 8, or read the lyrics aloud. If students are able, have them recite the beat along with the CD or with you. Encourage students to use hand and body motions that correspond to the lyrics.

# IDENTIFY

teeth
_____
- - - - - - - - - - - - - - - - -
_____

lips
_____
- - - - - - - - - - - - - - - - -
_____

tongue
_____
- - - - - - - - - - - - - - - - -
_____

chin
_____
- - - - - - - - - - - - - - - - -
_____

toes
- - - - - - - - - - - - - - - - -
_____

ankle
_____
- - - - - - - - - - - - - - - - -
_____

knee
_____
- - - - - - - - - - - - - - - - -
_____

fingers
_____
- - - - - - - - - - - - - - - - -
_____

shoulder
_____
- - - - - - - - - - - - - - - - -
_____

back
_____
- - - - - - - - - - - - - - - - -
_____

wrist
_____
- - - - - - - - - - - - - - - - -
_____

elbow
_____

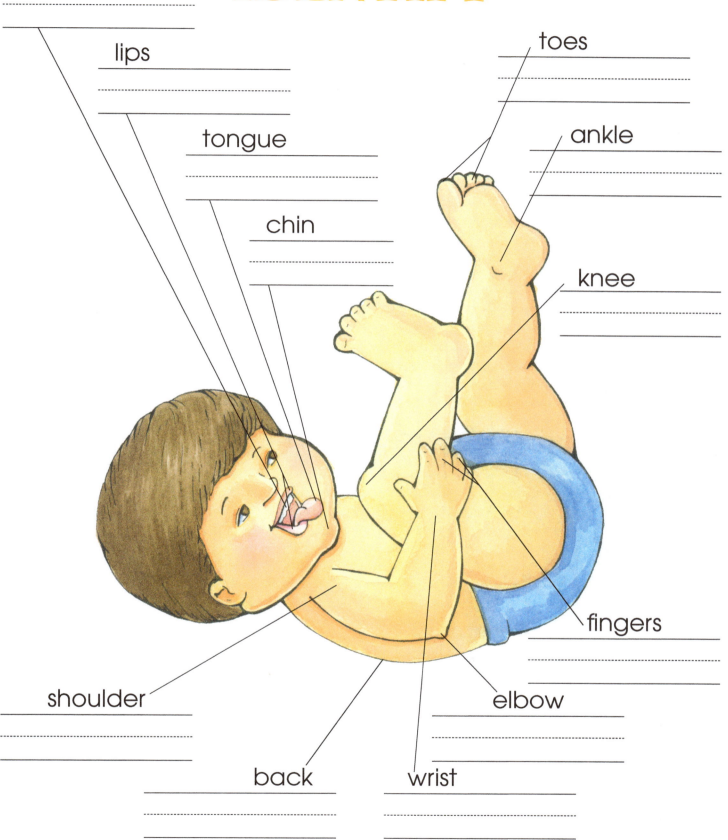

**Teacher:** Instruct students to identify and write the names of the body parts.

# CLASSIFY

## What goes together? Circle the pictures.

fingers

knee

nurse

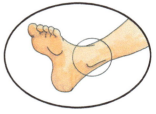

ankle

pear

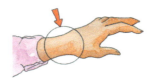

wrist

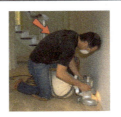

back

chin

shoulder

cat

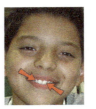

teeth

lips

glue

elbow

toes

tongue

They are all ___body parts___.

**Teacher:** Instruct students to circle the pictures on the page that go together. Then have students write the words below the pictures they have circled.

58

# MATCH UP

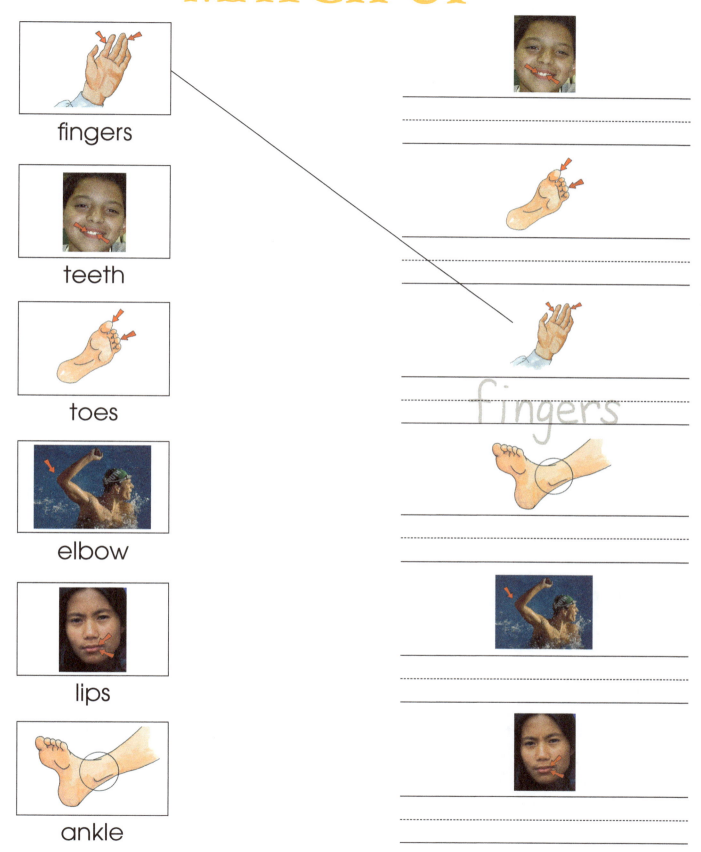

**fingers**

**teeth**

**toes**

**elbow**

**lips**

**ankle**

fingers

**Teacher:** Instruct students to draw lines to connect the matching pictures, and then write the words.

# CUT UP

1. This is a **back**.

2. This is a **tongue**.

3. This is a **chin**.

4. This is a **shoulder**.

5. This is a **wrist**.

6. This is a **knee**.

**Teacher:** Instruct students to cut out each picture, and paste it in the box next to the sentence it matches.

Copyright ©2007 by Ballard & Tighe, Publishers, a division of Educational IDEAS, Inc. All rights reserved. No part of this publication may be reproduced in any form or by any means, electronic or mechanical, including photocopy, recording, or any information storage and retrieval system, without permission in writing from the publisher.

# MATCH UP

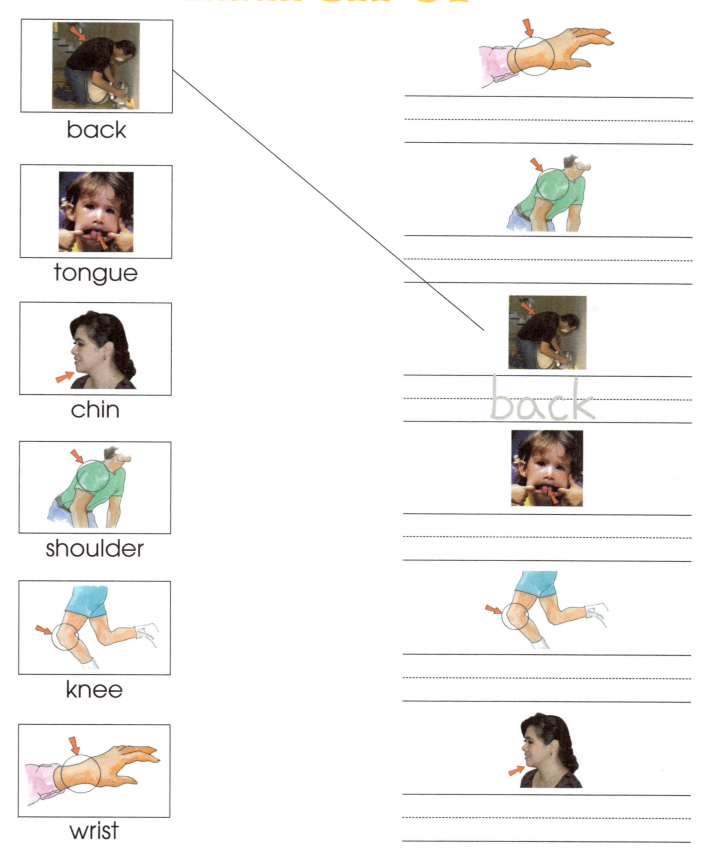

back

tongue

chin

shoulder

knee

wrist

back

**Teacher:** Instruct students to draw lines to connect the matching pictures, and then write the words.

# REVIEW

Listen,  Repeat, and Write

These are shapes.

1.      It's a **triangle**.

_____

2.      It's a **square**.

_____

## Make the sentences:

3. line _____

4. circle _____

5. rectangle _____

These are parts of the body.

6.      This is an **ankle**.

_____

7.      This is an **elbow**.

_____

**Teacher:** Instruct students to listen to, repeat, and write the sentences. Use the Book 2 CD, Track 7, or have students repeat after you. **If using the CD, press the pause button when you hear the beep and instruct students to write the sentence or key word. When students are finished writing, resume the CD.** For items 3–5, 9–12, and 14–16, students create their own sentences orally, but write the key words only.

# REVIEW

Listen, Repeat, and Write

8.     This is a **back**.

## Make the sentences:

9. tongue     10. shoulder     11. knee     12. wrist

13.     These are **fingers**.

## Make the sentences:

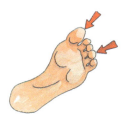         

14. toes     15. lips     16. teeth

# IDENTIFY

on top of

off

upside down

up

next to

down

inside

outside

away from

behind

in order

in a row

**Teacher:** Instruct students to identify and write the spatial positions.

# BUILD UP

## Listen  and Repeat

1.  It is **on top of** the table.

2. He climbs **up** the ladder.

3.  He jumps **down**.

4.  She is **inside** the box.

5.  He jumps **off**.

6.  He is **upside down**.

*(continued on next page)*

**Teacher:** Instruct students to listen to and repeat the sentences. Use the <u>Book 2 CD, Track 9</u>, or have students repeat after you.

# BUILD UP

## Listen  and Repeat

7.  She is **outside** the box.

8.  He is **beside** the table.

9.  He runs **away from** her.

10.  He puts them **in order**.

11.  They stand **in a row**.

12.  He is **behind** the tree.

# MATCH UP

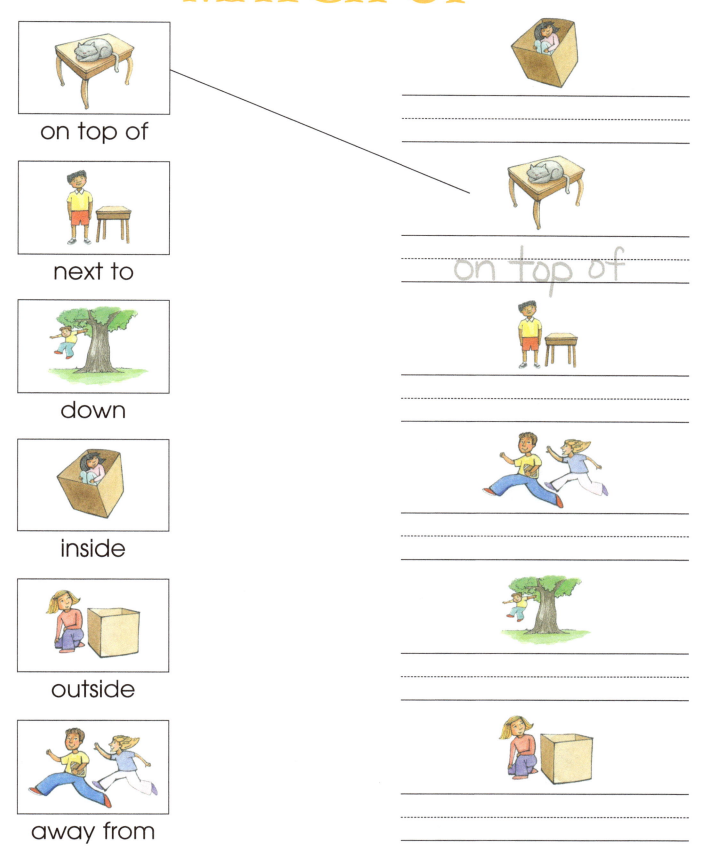

on top of

next to

down

inside

outside

away from

on top of

**Teacher:** Instruct students to draw lines to connect the matching pictures, and then write the words.

# CUT UP

1. He climbs **up** the ladder.

2. He jumps **off** the ladder.

3. He is **behind** the tree.

4. He puts them **in order**.

5. They stand **in a row**.

6. He hangs **upside down**.

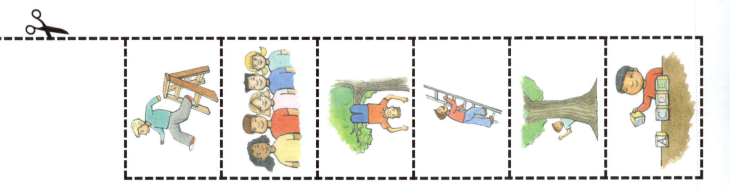

**Teacher:** Instruct students to cut out each picture, and paste it in the box next to the sentence it matches.

# MATCH UP

behind

in order

up

off

in a row

upside down

behind

**Teacher:** Instruct students to draw lines to connect the matching pictures, and then write the words.

# REVIEW

Listen, 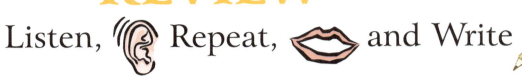 Repeat, and Write

1. It is **on top of** the table.

2. He climbs **up** the ladder.

3. He jumps **down**.

4. She is **inside** the box.

5. He jumps **off**.

6. He is **upside down**.

**Teacher:** Instruct students to listen to, repeat, and write the sentences. Use the Book 2 CD, Track 9, or have students repeat after you. If using the CD, press the pause button when you hear the beep and instruct students to write the sentence or key word. When students are finished writing, resume the CD.

70

# REVIEW

Listen,  Repeat, and Write

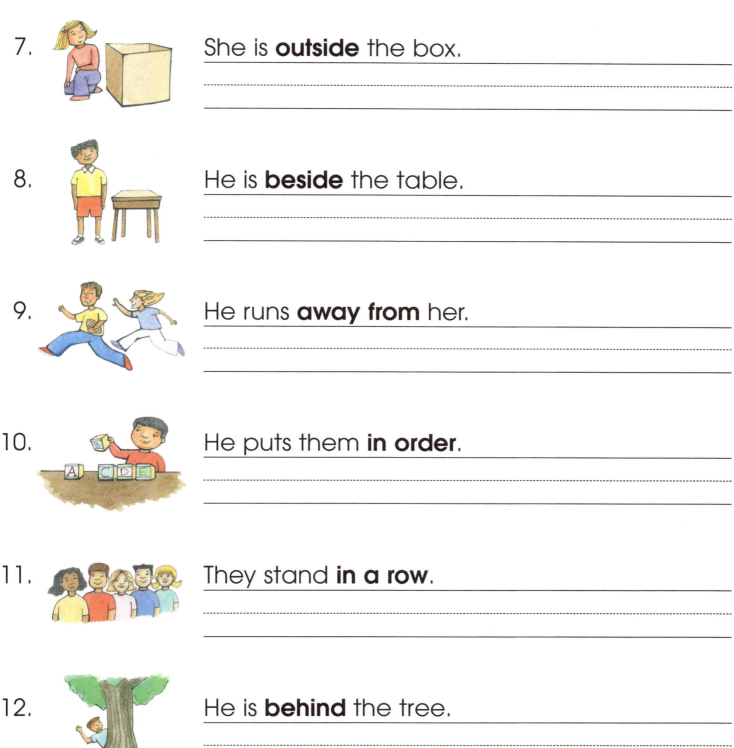

7. She is **outside** the box.

8. He is **beside** the table.

9. He runs **away from** her.

10. He puts them **in order**.

11. They stand **in a row**.

12. He is **behind** the tree.

# IDENTIFY

# Please ...

cut

glue

fold

point

color

write

**Teacher:** Instruct students to identify and write the commands.

# BUILD UP

Listen,  Repeat,  and Do

1.  **Draw** a circle.

2.  **Color** the circle.

3. **Cut out** the circle.

4. **Glue** the circle on your paper.

5.  **Draw a line** under the circle.

6.  **Put an X** on the line.

7.  **Fold** the paper.

8.  **Write** your name on the paper.

9.  **Point** to your name.

**Teacher:** Instruct students to listen to and repeat each sentence and then follow the command using the <u>Book 2 CD, Track 10</u>, or have students repeat after you. **If using the CD, press the pause button when you hear the beep and instruct students to follow the command. When students are finished with the task, resume the CD.** Students will need a pencil, crayon, scissors, glue, and two sheets of paper.

# CUT UP

1.  Please **write** your name.

2.  Please **color** the picture.

3.  Please **cut** out the circle.

4.  Please **fold** the paper.

5.  Please **glue**.

6.  Please **point** to the door.

✂ - - - - - - - - - - - - - - - - - - - - - - - - - - - - - - - - - - -

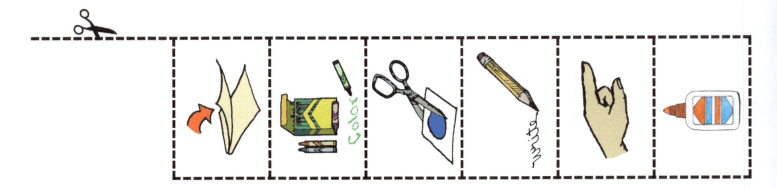

**Teacher:** Instruct students to cut out each picture, and paste it in the box next to the sentence it matches.

# MATCH UP

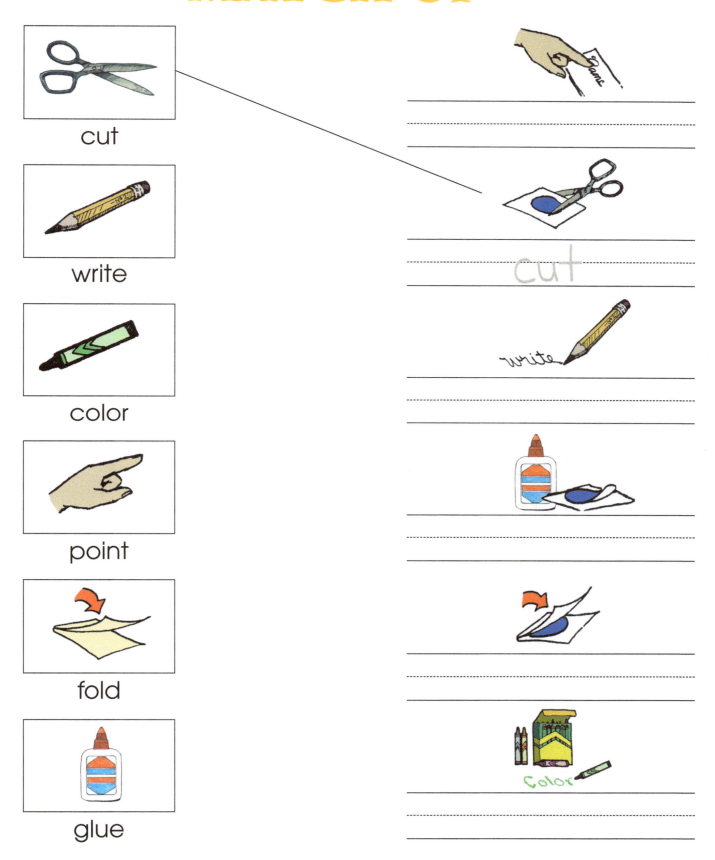

cut

write

color

point

fold

glue

cut

write

Color

**Teacher:** Instruct students to draw lines to connect the pictures that go together, and then write the words.

# REVIEW

Listen,  Repeat,  and Write

1. **Draw** a circle.

_____

2. **Color** the circle.

_____

3. **Cut out** the circle.

_____

4. **Glue** the circle on your paper.

_____

5. **Draw a line** under the circle.

_____

6. **Put an X** on the line.

_____

7. **Fold** the paper.

_____

8. **Write** your name on the paper.

_____

9. **Point** to your name.

_____

**Teacher:** Instruct students to listen to, repeat, and write the sentences. Use the Book 2 CD, Track 10, or have students repeat after you. **If using the CD, press the pause button when you hear the beep and instruct students to write the sentence or key word. When students are finished writing, resume the CD.**

# IDENTIFY

1. Is this a book?     **yes** (**no**)

2. Do monkeys go to school?     **yes**    **no**

3. Is the teacher a man?     **yes**    **no**

4. Does he have a nose?     **yes**    **no**

5. Can you eat a chair?     **yes**    **no**

6. Is this a banana?     **yes**    **no**

7. Can you eat an apple?     **yes**    **no**

8. Does it have three ears?     **yes**    **no**

**Teacher:** Instruct students on the concepts of "yes" and "no." Read each sentence to students, and have them circle the appropriate response.

# YES OR NO?

1.  Is the  in the bowl? _____ yes

2.  Is the in the bowl? _____ no

3.  Is the in the bowl? _____

4.  Is the in the bowl? _____

5.  Is the in the bowl? _____

6.  Is the in the bowl? _____

7.  Is the in the bowl? _____

**Teacher:** Instruct students to look at the picture, and then write "yes" or "no" as appropriate.

# YES OR NO?

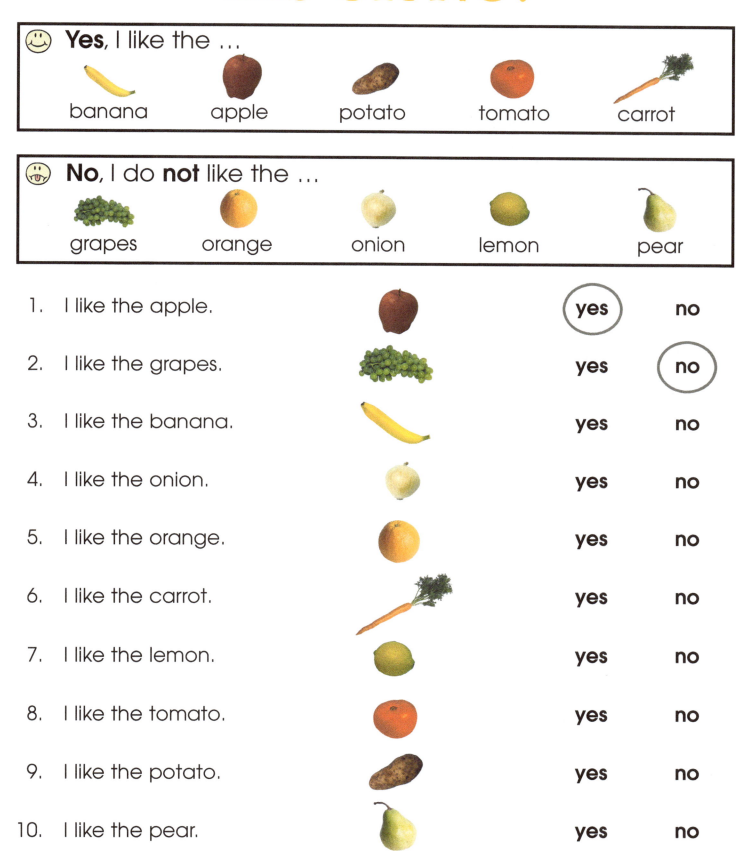

☺ **Yes**, I like the …

banana   apple   potato   tomato   carrot

☹ **No**, I do **not** like the …

grapes   orange   onion   lemon   pear

1. I like the apple.    yes    no

2. I like the grapes.    yes    no

3. I like the banana.    yes    no

4. I like the onion.    yes    no

5. I like the orange.    yes    no

6. I like the carrot.    yes    no

7. I like the lemon.    yes    no

8. I like the tomato.    yes    no

9. I like the potato.    yes    no

10. I like the pear.    yes    no

**Teacher:** Instruct students to study the charts at the top of the page, and then answer the questions by circling "yes" or "no."

# IDENTIFY

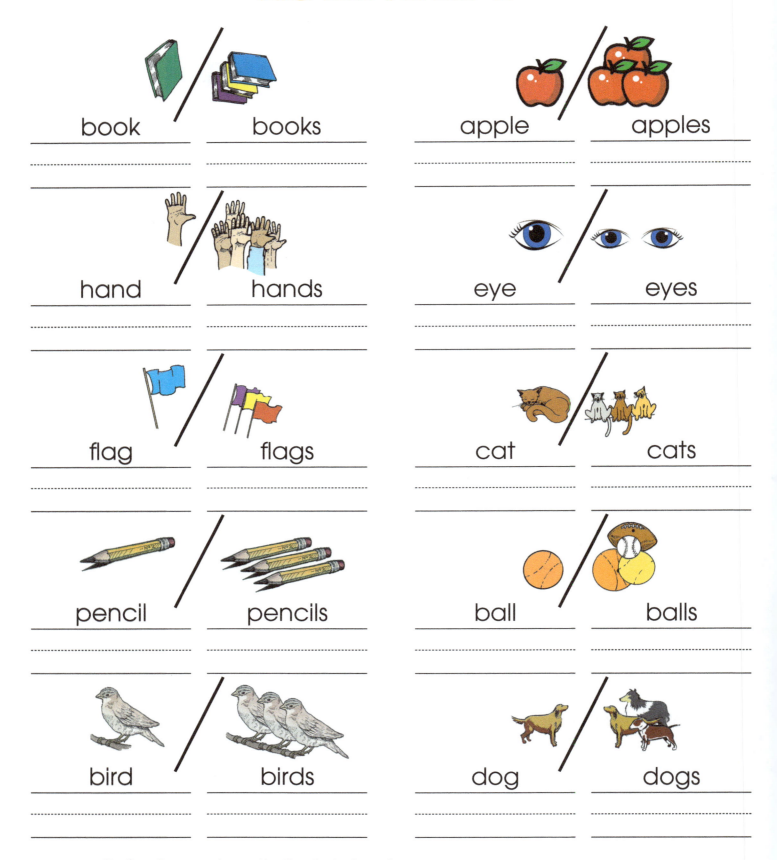

book   /   books

apple   /   apples

hand   /   hands

eye   /   eyes

flag   /   flags

cat   /   cats

pencil   /   pencils

ball   /   balls

bird   /   birds

dog   /   dogs

**Teacher:** Instruct students to identify and write the words.

# BUILD UP

## Listen  and Repeat

1. This is a **book**.

   These are **books**.

2. This is a **bird**.

   These are **birds**.

3. This is a **flag**.

   These are **flags**.

4. This is a **pencil**.

   These are **pencils**.

5. This is a **hand**.

   These are **hands**.

*(continued on next page)*

**Teacher:** Instruct students to listen to and repeat the sentences. Use the <u>Book 2 CD, Track 11</u>, or have students repeat after you.

# BUILD UP

Listen 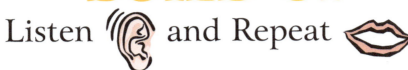 and Repeat

6. This is a **cat**.

These are **cats**.

7. This is a **ball**.

These are **balls**.

8. This is a **dog**.

These are **dogs**.

9. This is an **eye**.

These are **eyes**.

10. This is an **apple**.

These are **apples**.

# MATCH UP

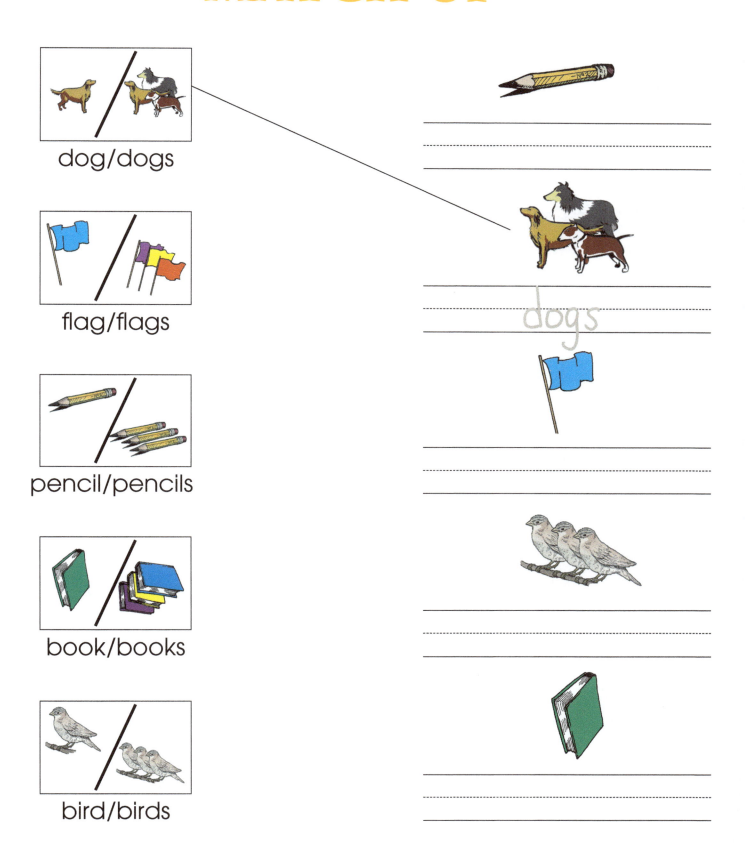

dog/dogs

flag/flags

pencil/pencils

book/books

bird/birds

dogs

**Teacher:** Instruct students to draw lines to connect the pictures that go together, and then write the appropriate singular or plural words.

# CUT UP

1. This is an **apple**.

2. These are **eyes**.

3. These are **balls**.

4. This is a **cat**.

5. These are **hands**.

✂ - - - - - - - - - - - - - - - - - - - - - - - - - - - - - - - - - - - - -

**Teacher:** Instruct students to cut out each picture, and paste it in the box next to the sentence it matches.

# MATCH UP

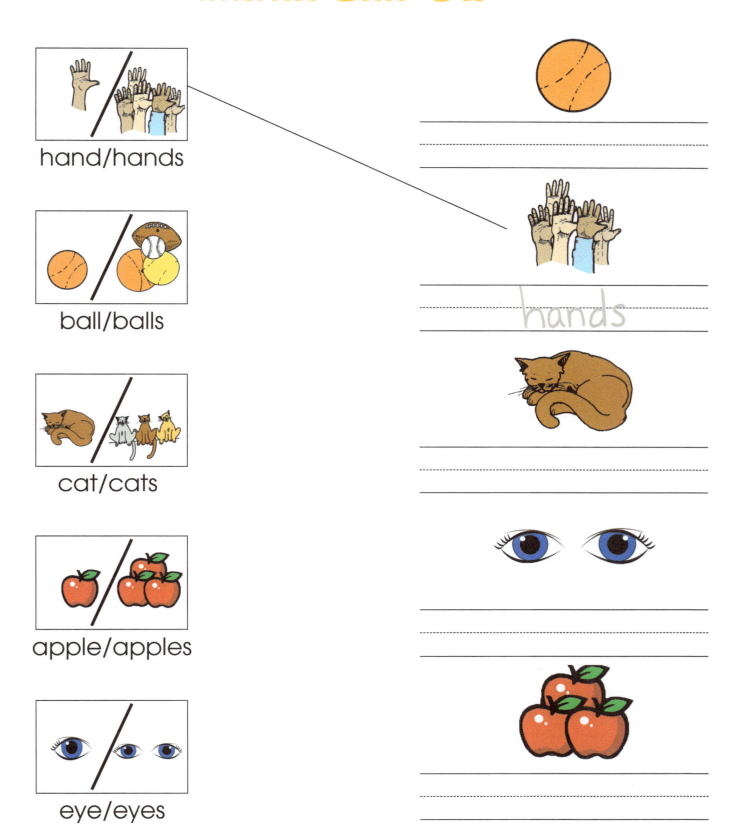

hand/hands

ball/balls

cat/cats

apple/apples

eye/eyes

hands

**Teacher:** Instruct students to draw lines to connect the pictures that go together, and then write the appropriate singular or plural words.

# REVIEW

 11 Listen,  Repeat,  and Write

1.   This is a **book**.

  These are **books**.

2.   This is a **bird**.

These are **birds**.

3.   This is a **flag**.

  These are **flags**.

4.   This is a **pencil**.

  These are **pencils**.

5.   This is a **hand**.

  These are **hands**.

**Teacher:** Instruct students to listen to, repeat, and write the sentences. Use the Book 2 CD, Track 11, or have students repeat after you. If using the CD, press the pause button when you hear the beep and instruct students to write the sentence or key word. When students are finished writing, resume the CD.

# REVIEW

Listen,   Repeat,  and Write

**6.**

This is a **cat**.

_____

These are **cats**.

_____

**7.**

This is a **ball**.

_____

These are **balls**.

_____

**8.**

This is a **dog**.

_____

These are **dogs**.

_____

**9.**

This is an **eye**.

_____

These are **eyes**.

_____

**10.**

This is an **apple**.

_____

These are **apples**.

_____

# IDENTIFY

I

you

we

he

she

it

they

**Teacher:** Instruct students to identify and write the pronouns.

# BUILD UP
## Listen  and Repeat

1.  **We** are in school.

2.  **I** am working.

3.  **It** is a circle.

4.  **You** are here.

5.  **They** are children.

6.  **He** is a boy.

7.  **She** is a girl.

**Teacher:** Instruct students to listen to and repeat the sentences. Use the <u>Book 2 CD, Track 12</u>, or have students repeat after you.

# CUT UP

1. **I** am in school.

2. **He** wants to go.

3. **She** likes to play.

4. **We** are here.

5. **You** are working.

6. **It** is round.

7. **They** are happy.

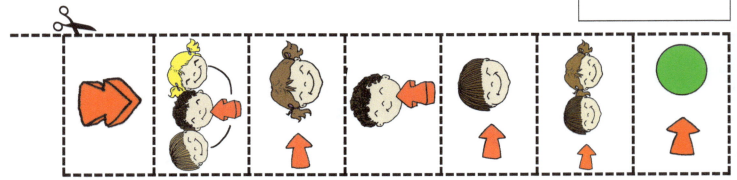

**Teacher:** Instruct students to cut out each picture, and paste it in the box next to the sentence it matches.

# MATCH UP

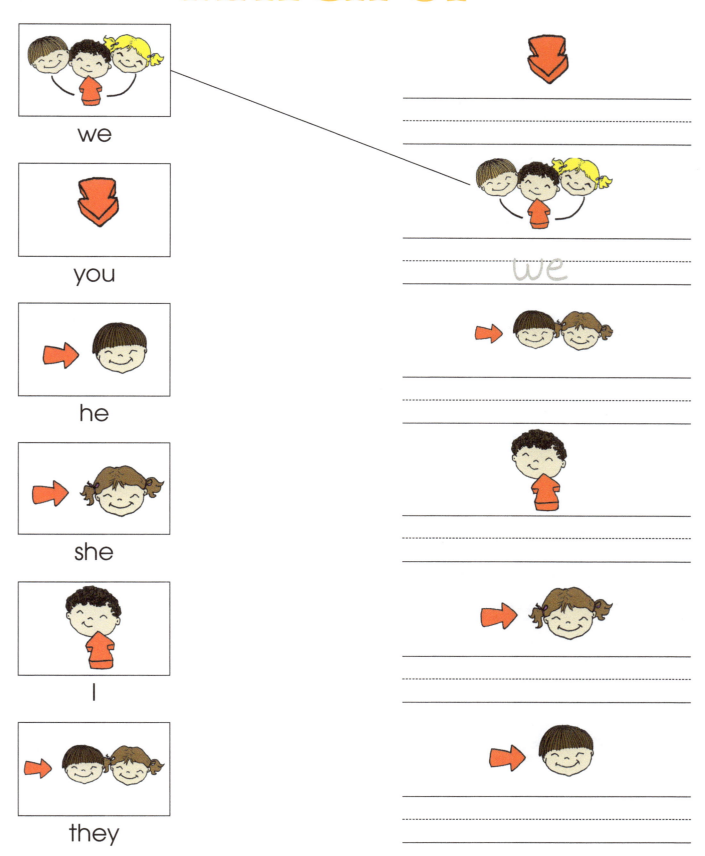

we

you

he

she

I

they

we

**Teacher:** Instruct students to draw lines to connect the matching pictures, and then write the words.

# REVIEW

Listen,  Repeat, and Write

1. **We** are in school.

2. **I** am working.

3. **It** is a circle.

4. **You** are here.

5. **They** are children.

6. **He** is a boy.

7. **She** is a girl.

**Teacher:** Instruct students to listen to, repeat, and write the sentences. Use the Book 2 CD, Track 12, or have students repeat after you. If using the CD, press the pause button when you hear the beep and instruct students to write the sentence or key word. When students are finished writing, resume the CD.

# BUILD UP

Listen and Repeat

1.  m      <u>m</u>an      ma<u>m</u>a      na<u>m</u>e

2.  n      <u>n</u>o       fu<u>nn</u>y     fa<u>n</u>

3.  p      <u>p</u>an      ha<u>pp</u>y     to<u>p</u>

4.  h      <u>h</u>at      be<u>h</u>ind    ~

5.  w      <u>w</u>ork     side<u>w</u>alk  ~

6.  b      <u>b</u>oy      ra<u>bb</u>it    we<u>b</u>

*(continued on next page)*

**Teacher:** Instruct students to listen to and repeat the sounds, words, and sentences. Use the <u>Book 2 CD, Track 13</u>, or have students repeat after you.

7.   k        king        turkey        rock

8.   g        game        tiger         dog

9.   f        foot        coffee        leaf

10.  y        yes         onion         ~

11.  ng       ~           singer        ring

12.  d        duck        candy         head

13.  The boy is **under the table**.

14.  The puppy is **in the box**.

15.  This is **for the cat**.

16.  The tree is **between the girls**.

17.  The pencil is **beside the book**.

18.  The bird flew **over my head**.

*(continued on next page)*

# BUILD UP

CONSONANT SOUNDS &
AUDITORY MEMORY

Listen and Repeat

19.  We eat cake **after dinner**.

20.  This is **a big boat**.

21.  The man is **in front of the car**.

22.  This is **a little ball**.

23.  He runs **around the house**.

24.  Look at **the big tiger**.

# VERBAL EXPRESSION

What is she thinking about? Talk about three things. Use the PRESENT tense.

My name: _____

_____

_____

**Teacher:** Have students look at the pictures and create sentences using the simple present tense.

# IDENTIFY
## Where is the pencil?

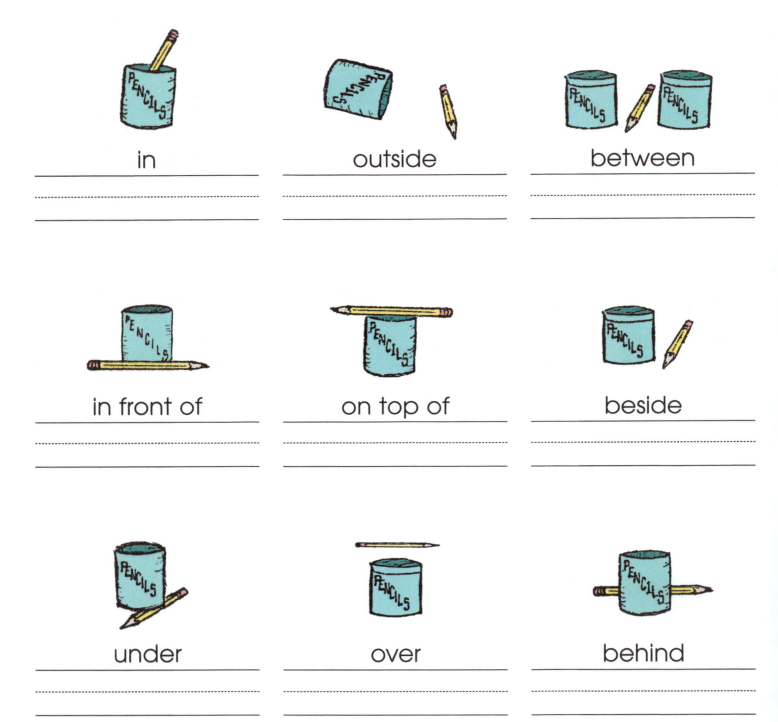

in

outside

between

in front of

on top of

beside

under

over

behind

**Teacher:** Instruct students to identify and write the location of the pencil.

# BUILD UP

1.  The pencil is **behind** the pencil holder.

2.  The pencil is **in front of** the pencil holder.

3.  The pencil is **in** the pencil holder.

4.  The pencil is **over** the pencil holder.

5.  The pencil is **on top of** the pencil holder.

6.  The pencil is **under** the pencil holder.

7.  The pencil is **outside** the pencil holder.

8.  The pencil is **between** two pencil holders.

9.  The pencil is **beside** the pencil holder.

**Teacher:** Provide students with pencils and pencil holders. Read each sentence. Have students repeat each sentence and move their pencils accordingly.

# ARTIST AT WORK

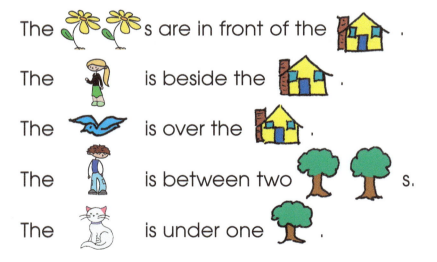

The 🌼🌼s are in front of the 🏠 .

The 👧 is beside the 🏠 .

The 🐦 is over the 🏠 .

The 🧍 is between two 🌳 s.

The 🐱 is under one 🌳 .

- Tell your teacher about your picture.

- Color your picture.

**Teacher:** Instruct students to draw the objects on the picture as directed in the above sentences.